YOUR 40 DAY JOURNEY

Getting Closer to God Each Day

Bev Hurlburt

WESTBOW
PRESS
A DIVISION OF THOMAS NELSON

WestBow Press books may be ordered through booksellers or by contacting:

WestBow Press
A Division of Thomas Nelson
1663 Liberty Drive
Bloomington, IN 47403
www.westbowpress.com
1-(866) 928-1240

ISBN: 978-1-4497-0947-1 (e)
ISBN: 978-1-4497-0949-5 (sc)

Library of Congress Control Number: 2010941834

Printed in the United States of America

WestBow Press rev. date: 1/14/2011

PREFACE

When my first husband died in 1999, I had no idea how a person would get through that kind of pain. I knew God, but had no idea what part He would play as I struggled with the grief. My oldest daughter, who was 14 when her dad died, had already given her life to the Lord. I would see her in her room at night reading a book on one side of her while she had the Bible opened up on the opposite side. One night I asked her what she was reading and she told me she was doing her devotion. I had no idea what that was and was too embarrassed to ask her. A few years later I was asked to teach Sunday school. That seemed far-fetched and out of the question because even though I had gone to church all of my life I had never read the Bible. I knew so little about the life that Jesus had lived. God prodded me to say yes to teaching junior high Sunday school and it was then that my faith began to grow. I studied scripture so that I could teach it to the students. I started loving the stories in the Bible and when our pastor offered a two-year Bible study class I jumped at the chance to learn as much as I could about the Father,

Son and Holy Spirit. My faith blossomed and flourished once I began to understand God's grace, His mercy and His unconditional love. Once I had read the Bible I was ready to accept the peace and joy that God grants us when we allow Him to work in our lives. It is so important that in order to live in this world but not be of this world we need to be in God's Word daily. I believe that we need to have a daily dose of His truth to sustain us through our everyday lives. The best way I found to do that was to have a devotion book to refer to every single morning. (My daughter chooses nighttime, I choose early morning and you might choose noon. The time does not matter. Daily is what's important.) My vision for this book is to provide the reader with a scripture to look up and study. The story included each day is my way of placing that scripture into our everyday lives.

Devoting time to God is the most important way to start and end each day. When you read each story and the subsequent scripture, I highly recommend that you stretch your reading to include the entire chapter of the Bible. Reading the chapter before and after the devotional scripture will only increase your knowledge of God's Word. (Each scripture is from the New Living Bible unless otherwise noted.)

There are no dates or days on each page, and this was done on purpose. It's your book. You can read it in any order you want. You can randomly open the book and read that devotional. You can read the first page, second page, third page, and so on in order. You can look at each devotional title and read the one that coincides with what's going on in your life at that moment. You can even read the end before the beginning. It's your choice.

I chose to write forty devotions for this book because of the numerous forty-day journeys that played significant roles in the Bible. When God wanted to cleanse the world, it rained for forty days and forty nights. Moses was on Mount Sinai for forty days when the Ten Commandments were written. Elijah went to Mount Horeb for forty days, and on that mountain, he heard the still, small voice of God. Jesus fasted for forty days in the wilderness. In His hunger, He was able to deny the devil's temptations. These forty-day journeys produced a dramatic change that brought each person involved closer to God. They committed to the challenge and in the end their love for the Lord increased and their faith was stronger. That is what I pray this book brings to you.

Great and wondrous events took place during these journeys of forty days. As you go into your forty-day journey, I pray you get the cleansing, the strength, and the direction you need. I pray you hear God's still, small voice speaking directly to you.

CONTENTS

GOD KNOWS BEST

This is what the Lord says—your Redeemer the Holy One of Israel:

"I am the Lord your God, who teaches you what is best for you, who directs you in the way you should go" (Isaiah 48:17).

God talks to each of us in different ways. He knows us so well—so personally—that He can speak our language. He allows us to hear Him in ways each one of us will understand.

Creativity has never come to me in an instant. When I have a project presented to me, I have to think about it and mull it over in my mind—perhaps even dwell on it for days at a time. I go through many images and scenarios until I'm able to sort through them to the perfect plan. It's in those moments of contemplation that God speaks to me. It's when I'm the most open-minded, most available to receive fresh ideas—His ideas. He may talk to you through music or opening the Bible and focusing on one Scripture, or perhaps He wakes you in the middle of the night with a profound thought. He will speak to you in the way you best understand.

But how do we know it's Him? God knows us intimately; it's time we get to know Him intimately in return. We need to be in the Bible—in God's Word—daily so His voice becomes the most familiar voice we hear and so we know how He sounds and how He communicates with us.

I don't know about you, but I want to hear God when He speaks to me. I want to know it's His voice so I can learn from Him what is best for me and I can go in the direction He wants me to go. My deepest desire is to have a personal and intimate relationship with my Father God, and the really cool thing is—that's exactly what He desires, too!

SHARING OUR FAITH

I long to see you so that I may impart to you some spiritual gift to make you strong—that is, that you and I may be mutually encouraged by each other's faith (Romans 1:11–12).

I have some amazing Christian girlfriends. Each one is unique, and each one has special, God-given gifts. In different ways, each one has shared her faith and convictions with me at a time when I have needed them so desperately. I pray I have done the same in return. We are made by God to be in relationships with others. We are made to encourage and to lift up one another.

There has been more than one occasion when I have been in great need of prayer and I know that as soon as I ask, my girlfriends will stop what they are doing and pray to our Heavenly Father. I can't begin to tell you the confidence in the Lord this gives me to know I have a band of prayer warriors eager to talk to God on my behalf.

One day as I was leaving for a weekend speaking engagement, Satan was attacking me with a vengeance. I sent out a mass request to my girlfriends for prayer. I want to share with you the written prayer I received as a text message on my phone:

> In the name of Jesus, Satan, leave now the mind, the thoughts, the car and, the entire area Bev will be in this weekend. Father, hold tight Your vessel, Bev, to speak tenderly and confidently without the bondage of the enemy. Lord, I ask You to continue to let Bev's love for You and the words she delivers to flow openly and with the passion needed to lift these people this weekend. Father, use Bev. She loves this mission field and wants to shine for You. What a blessing You have in her. In Your name, send Satan packin'. We love You, Jesus. Amen.

After I read this, I thanked God for my wonderful friends. Then I smiled and said to Satan, "Take that!"

HIS PLAN FOR YOU

*For we are God's workmanship, created in Christ Jesus
to do good works, which God prepared in advance for
us to do* (Ephesians 2:10).

That Scripture is powerful and empowering. For years, I thought I had no talents or gifts. Perhaps you've felt that way, or perhaps you feel that way now. I was not the best at anything. I had nothing special to offer. But this Scripture tells me that God created me in the image of His perfect Son, Jesus Christ. And after He created me, He compiled a "to do" list and placed my name at the top of it. And because He is a loving and gracious God, He equipped me with the necessary abilities I would need to complete those tasks.

And it's not just me He did this for; God has created each one of His children in the image of Jesus Christ. Each one of us has a "to do" list compiled by Him with our individual name on it. He already has a plan for you and for me. We simply need to submit to Him and to His will for us.

The day will come when you and I will come face-to-face with our Savior. This is what I pray will happen: He will look at each of us, He will look at our "to do" list, and He will say, "Well done, good and faithful servant."

WAIT FOR THE LORD

*Wait for the Lord; be strong and take heart and wait
for the Lord* (Psalm 27:14).

It seems that in the spring of the year is when I'm most
antsy. I want new things to happen, and I want them right
away! I don't know if it's because of the grass turning
green or the tulips blooming or because the sun shines
more often, but when the days begin getting nice and
longer, my mind goes in a million different directions. I
want to do everything—today!

Let's plant the flowers! Let's go fishing! Let's plan a
vacation! Let's go away this weekend! Let's have our friends
over for a barbeque! Let's take a bike ride! Let's wash the
windows—okay, so that never really enters the equation,
but you get the point. I get so excited, my adrenaline starts
flowing, and life can't move fast enough.

I have to remind myself that while being enthusiastic about
life is a good thing, I don't have to do everything in one

week. I need to relax, enjoy the sunshine, take in the smell of the freshly mowed grass, and marvel at the wonders of new blooms. I need to look for the Lord in all the beauty of a fresh season. I need to wait for the Lord to tell me each day what I can do to further His kingdom. If I fill each day with continuous activity, I may miss His plan for me. I certainly don't want to be washing windows when I could be visiting with a shut-in and building a new relationship. I don't want to miss one thing that God has planned for me. I will purposely choose to wait for the Lord.

GIVE YOUR PAIN TO GOD

Do not be anxious about anything, but in everything, by prayer and petition, with thanksgiving, present your requests to God. And the peace of God, which transcends all understanding, will guard your hearts and your minds in Christ Jesus (Philippians 4:6–7).

This verse tells you to take your worry, your hurt, your pain, and your anger to God in prayer and—here is the tough part—leave it with Him. Tell God, "Here You go; it's all Yours." Oh, if only it were that simple, right? Saying it is easy, but actually doing it certainly isn't. We start asking ourselves, "Doesn't God want me to deal with my own problems? Doesn't He want me to face my pain and deal with it?" Yes, He wants you to be able to cope with your burdens, but not on your own. He knows that the only way you will be able to manage that is through His strength, His grace, His mercy, and His love! Here's the deal: when you give your pain to God, that doesn't mean that He will pick you up and hurdle you over the problem. He doesn't want you to ignore it or let it linger and build. God begs you to turn your problems over to Him so He can give you the peace and the strength to get through them and come out on the other side in better shape and with stronger faith.

I was listening to a Christian radio station one day on my drive to work, and in the song that was playing, one particular sentence stuck out to me: "God will take away the pain—if you choose to let Him." Pain represents everything keeping you from His peace—hurt, loneliness, loss, rejection, anger. The list is different for each one of you. In order to live with the peace of God, which transcends all understanding, you must choose to go to Him through prayer and petition. You must choose to give your pain to God.

REST IS GIVEN

"Come to me, all you who are weary and burdened, and I will give you rest. Take my yoke upon you and learn from me, for I am gentle and humble in heart, and you will find rest for your souls. For my yoke is easy and my burden is light" (Matthew 11:28–30).

Take a deep breath in, hold it, and slowly let it out. Clear your mind, and let your body relax. Read the above Scripture in this paraphrased way, adding your name in the blanks.

> "Come to Me, _____, when you are weary and burdened, and I, Jesus, will give you rest. Take My yoke upon you, _____, and learn from Me, for I am gentle and humble in heart, and you will find rest for your soul. For My yoke is easy, and My burden is light. Remember how much My Father and I love you, _____."

This is Jesus, our Lord and Savior, speaking to you.

Jesus is asking—no, He is begging—you to come to Him when you are tired and filled with anxiety and stress. Instead of trying to be strong and courageous in order to get through it on your own, you need to stop, admit you are tired, and ask Jesus to trade your burden for His peace and for rest in Him. Only when you take His yoke upon you and learn from Him will you find rest for your soul.

YOUR FUTURE WITH GOD

"For I know the plans I have for you," declares the Lord, "plans to prosper you and not to harm you, plans to give you hope and a future. Then you will call upon me and come and pray to me, and I will listen to you. You will seek me and find me when you seek me with all your heart" (Jeremiah 29:11–13).

I feel unbelievably confidant and strong knowing that God has a plan for me. It relieves me to know that He is in control. Think about it—the creator of the universe, the alpha and the omega, the beginning and the end, the great I AM has plans to prosper me, and He has plans to prosper you. He asks in return only that we call on Him in prayer and seek Him with our hearts. He asks for so little, and He gives us so much. We are Yours, God—have Your will in us. He has already thought about our days. He has already laid out the roadmap. His plans for us include hope and a future. Our plan should be to seek Him every day with all our hearts so that we can find Him and say yes to whatever it is He has planned for us.

Reading and studying God's word allows us to accept several things:

- God is good
- God is love
- God loves us unconditionally
- God wants what is best for us
- God made us on purpose
- God never backs down on His promise
- God will always be with us
- God listens to us when we pray
- God's timing is perfect
- God has great plans for our future

It is so important to read Scripture each day. This is the only way to know how truly wonderful our Heavenly Father is and to know that we can depend on Him to prosper us and not harm us—to give us hope and a future.

TOUGH TIMES

And we know that in all things God works for the good of those who love Him, who have been called according to His purpose (Romans 8:28).

My first husband died suddenly of a massive heart attack at the age of forty-two. We had been married eighteen years, and our daughters were fourteen and ten years old. I had the husband other women wished they had. He was involved with our daughters and missed very little of what was going in their lives. My husband and I were always side by side, enjoying our children together.

What good could ever come from tearing our family apart? We had worked so hard to make our marriage work when so many were falling apart around us.

Ten years later, I am remarried to another wonderful man. More importantly, I have grown intensely close to our Heavenly Father. I talk to Him daily. He is a constant presence in my life. Since 2008, I have had the pleasure and the joy to speak about God at worship services, church gatherings, and women's retreats. I have had the great privilege of witnessing to others about how God has brought me to the other side of grief to love and laugh again.

I am a walking, breathing, living example of Romans 8:28. For we know that in all things God works for the good of those who love Him and are called according to His purpose.

Dear Father God, I love everything You have done in my life. Thank You for never leaving me. Thank You for the strength You have provided for me through Your Holy Spirit. Amen.

REBUKE SATAN

So do not throw away your confidence, it will be richly rewarded. You need to persevere so that when you have done the will of God, you will receive what He has promised (Hebrews 10:35–36).

I cannot begin to tell you how hard Satan has worked this year to shake my confidence. It's with a heavy heart that I tell you there were many times he nearly succeeded in convincing me that I was not wise enough, good enough, or important enough to speak in front of a group and share my love for Christ.

Thank goodness for my prayer partners. I send out text messages and tell them Satan is at it again, and they stop what they are doing and pray for me. I joyously tell you that each time I have rebuked Satan, my confidence soars. God richly rewarded me every time I said, "Satan, I will *not* listen to you! My God is bigger than you, and I will hold on to my confidence, because my confidence comes from knowing God and His Son, Jesus Christ. I want to receive what God has promised me—so Satan, you are *not* welcome in my life!"

I know that God is seeing and hearing me deny Satan's attempt to throw me off course. I know it pleases Him. I imagine God smiling, elbowing Jesus as He points at me and says, "That's our girl!"

Tell Satan today—in no uncertain terms—that you will not allow him to destroy your confidence. And be prepared for God to supply you with more confidence than you ever imagined.

GOD LOVES A CELEBRATION

Celebrate this as a festival to the Lord for seven days each year. This is to be a lasting ordinance for the generations to come, celebrate it in the seventh month (Leviticus 23:41).

I love going to wedding receptions that my entire family is invited to. These receptions are nights of dining together, toasting the happy couple, and dancing. I love to dance with my husband and kids. We get in a circle and do silly things one by one in the middle. As much as I enjoy participating, I enjoy sitting and watching my children and their significant others having a good time. I get a smile on my face without even realizing it.

God smiles when we celebrate. Being a Christian brings marvelous reasons to celebrate each and every day. I remember when I first realized being a Christian is fun. Believe it or not, it was not that long ago. Our church Mission Team was planning a pizza party and talent show on a Saturday night. The talent show consisted of comedy, singing, music, and drama, and at the end of it all, the Mission Team performed a fun dance routine to Selah's "Deep," a lively, upbeat song about having the joy, peace, and love of Jesus. The place went wild! Everyone—young and old—was on their feet. They were clapping and cheering and laughing. God was watching His children dance and have fun together, and He was smiling!

CHRIST IN YOU

I have been crucified with Christ and I no longer live, but Christ lives in me. The life I live in the body, I live by faith in the Son of God, who loved me and gave Himself for me (Galatians 2:20).

As children of God, we get the full benefit of being crucified with Christ without the pain that He had to endure.

I sometimes sit, close my eyes, and picture Jesus being whipped and spit on. I imagine Him carrying the heavy cross, having the crown of thorns placed roughly on his head, and his hands and feet being nailed to the cross. I try hard to picture his body sweating pools of blood. I don't ever want to minimize the pain Jesus endured or the humiliation He went through for you and me.

I want to be that unselfish, loving, and giving—and the only way I can is to deny myself, my feelings, and my hurts and allow Christ to live in me. By remembering Christ's suffering, I remember that there is nothing He wouldn't do for me. It's then easy to put total faith in our Savior.

Have you heard of breath prayers? They are short prayers you can pray throughout the day as you inhale and exhale. You are welcome to use my breath prayer if you don't have one.

Inhale and say, "More of you, Lord." Exhale and say, "Less of me." More of you, Lord; less of me.

LOVE, NOT JUDGMENT

Therefore let us stop passing judgment on one another. Instead make up your mind not to put any stumbling block or obstacle in your brother's way (Romans 14:13).

Years ago, I read an autobiography of one of my favorite entertainers. In her book, she let the reader know she was married and had been for many years. She also insinuated—pretty clearly, actually—that she had "encounters" with other men—but she always returned home to her husband whom she loved dearly. I had a difficult time digesting that information. My opinion of her began to fade immediately. I thought, *I can't like this woman anymore. I can't listen to her music. She may donate a lot of money for wonderful causes, but she is a sinner.*

A day or two after I finished the book, God opened my ears to Him as He said, "It's not your place to judge." I felt such relief. I could still enjoy her talents and could enjoy the sweet disposition she portrayed when being interviewed. I could still be thankful for the money she spent on worthwhile missions—but the judging would not come from me. That would be between her soul, her heart, and God.

I am reminded often that it's not my place to judge. I, too, am a sinner who needs God's grace. Jesus is the only one worthy to cast the first stone. It is my place to hate the sin but love and pray for the sinner. It's my place to show the light of Christ to everyone I encounter. Once I realized this, it made it so much easier to love my neighbor. It's not up to me to judge.

GROW IN CHRIST

Make every effort to add to your faith goodness, and to your goodness, knowledge, and to knowledge, self-control and to self-control, perseverance, and to perseverance, godliness, and to godliness, brotherly kindness and to brotherly kindness, love (2 Peter 1:5–7).

To me, this sums up our desired journey with Christ. We don't stop by saying, "I have faith." Instead, through that faith we absorb what Jesus did for us and we allow His goodness to sink into our souls. We begin to read the Bible so that we truly understand the sacrifice He made, and we gather knowledge and realize the extent of His love for us. As we grow in knowledge, we recognize that because God loves us so much and because Jesus suffered so incredibly, we want to do and say what is pleasing to the Lord. Because this is new territory for us, we must use self-control to form new habits.

As soon as Satan sees that we are arming ourselves with knowledge and practicing self-control to please the Lord, then he starts his attack—tempting us with our own sinful nature. Through God's love and our new knowledge, we persevere and continue to obey God. Each time we obey Him and deny Satan, we inherit godliness. The next step in our journey is Christ-like kindness. Once we understand our Heavenly Father and what He wants from us and for us, we find goodness in everyone we meet. As we extend kindness to those close to us—and to our enemies—we develop love for others, just as Jesus loves us.

We become a child of God in an instant. It takes a lifelong journey to fulfill His command for us to love our neighbors as ourselves.

OBEY HIS WORD

Anyone who listens to the Word but does not do what it says is like a man who looks at his face in a mirror and after looking at himself, goes away and immediately forgets what he looks like (James 1:23–24).

Reading the Bible every day doesn't automatically make us Christians. Reading the Bible everyday *and* believing it is true *and* living as the Word calls us to live is what makes us Christians. Reading the Bible and not putting it into action is what makes us hypocrites.

I love God, and I am so thankful for our Savior, Jesus Christ. Why is it so difficult to live the way Jesus lived? Why do I continue to pass judgment? Why do I overlook the needs of the less fortunate and buy something to make my life more comfortable? Why do I not eat right, exercise, and take care of my body—even though I know that it is God's temple and that He uses my body to do His work?

I have a quote on my desk at work. It says, "Be careful how you live; you may be the only Bible some people read." I look at that all day long. I realize that if I intend to call myself a Christian, I should act like one. I need to put my hurt feelings and selfish desires aside and live the way the Bible tells me to live. James goes on to tell us in verse 25, "but the man who looks intently into the perfect law that gives freedom, and continues to do this, not forgetting what he has heard, but doing it—he will be blessed in what he does." And being blessed by God is a blessing indeed!

TRUST IN GOD

I will say of the Lord, "He is my refuge and my fortress, my God in whom I trust" (Psalm 91:2).

Trust—that's a biggie. What does it mean to trust in God? I've read the book; I know He is real. I know God is always with me and that He never leaves me nor forsakes me. Sure, I trust God. Would I trust Him like Abraham did when God asked Him to sacrifice his only son, Isaac? Would I trust Him like Noah did when he spent years and years building an ark that made people think he was crazy? Would I trust Him like Joseph, Jacob's son? His brothers sold him into slavery; he was thrown into prison for something he didn't do—and through it all, he continued to trust in the Lord. Or is my trust limited like that of Peter, who took one step in the water and then began to doubt?

Many times I entered into a dark period, and for a while, I trusted God. I knew He was there, and my faith could not be shaken. As the situation lingered and the circumstances got tougher, I would start to back away from my faith. I started thinking that maybe this would be the time that God would be too busy for me and want me to take care of things by myself. When the dark period was over and I made it through, I would look back and realize God had been with me the entire time. He was my source of strength and hope.

Each time this happens, we are a step closer to trusting God completely in every situation. We are one step closer to proclaiming—without a doubt—"He is my refuge and my fortress, my God in whom I trust."

LET GO OF ANGER

My dear brothers, take note of this: Everyone should be quick to listen, slow to speak and slow to become angry, for man's anger does not bring about the righteous life that God desires (James 1:19–20).

I've learned that giving my life to God doesn't mean that I am without problems and without sin. It means I need to trust Him to get me through the difficult situations and to repent of my sins so that He can offer me grace and forgiveness. I've learned that we all have the choice to be angry. Each one of us has had something happen in our life that was unfair and unjust. We have had the right to be angry. We hold on to our anger because we feel like we deserve to hold on to it. We say things like, "I'm a good person; I try to do the right thing" or "this should never have happened to me; it's not fair." Our friends and family will say, "I don't blame you; I'd be angry, too." But do you know what the high cost of holding on to anger is? It's living without joy. That's what we give up when we choose to be angry. We cannot have anger and joy in our hearts at the same time—there is not enough room. It's a choice we must make.

In listening to people, I find that in order for them to give up their anger, they have a list of things that need to change first. That list almost never includes them changing in any way.

When I remarried and had a blended family, the adjustment was extremely difficult at first. When I prayed for things to get better, I would always give God a list of ways He could change everyone around me so that my life would be better. The anger didn't subside until I asked God to change *me* and let *me* be more loving.

The freedom from anger starts when we pray to God to soften our hearts. It starts with being slow to speak and slow to become angry, and it continues when we live the righteous life that God desires.

LOVE WITHOUT CONDITIONS

But God demonstrates His own love for us in this: While we were still sinners, Christ died for us (Romans 5:8).

God didn't wait for us to be sin-free before He loved us. God didn't demand us to be without sin in order to receive His mercy, grace, and forgiveness. God meets us wherever we are, already loving us unconditionally, offering us His Son as our Savior to free us from our sins.

I don't ever want to stop being amazed at God's greatness. I don't ever want to forget the perfect sacrifice in Jesus Christ and the pain He suffered for me.

It is equally important to remember that I'm here on this earth to live a life that is as close to Jesus' life as humanly possible. Therefore, I need to love everyone—even those who appear to be unlovable. I need to offer grace to those who don't know God and to those who do. I need to offer forgiveness to those who have hurt and offended me or those who have deserted and abandoned me.

God, our Creator, the Lord over all, didn't wait for us to be perfect to offer us His Son. Who are we to place conditions on our grace, love, and forgiveness?

KNOW GOD

I don't want your sacrifices, I want your love. I don't want your offerings—I want you to know me (Hosea 6:6, TLB).

God's deepest desire may not be for our sacrifices, but He knows that sacrifice will come when we love Him. Our offerings are not as important to God as knowing Him; but when we know Him, our offerings will pour out.

How do we get to know God and love God when we can't see Him or touch Him? If only we could sit down with God for a cup of coffee.

It would be so easy to get acquainted with Him if He would come to dinner and answer all of our questions.

Here is the answer to getting to know God. It's a simple answer with few rules to follow. Are you ready for the surefire way to get to know God? Here it is: read the Bible daily.

We try so many avenues to get to know God. We listen to sermons and testimonies. We attend retreats and read self-help books. These are essential and wonderful ways to reinforce what we learn from His Word. But getting to know God must begin with the Bible. That's where we find out that He is with us during every cup of coffee, at every dinner, and during every moment in between. By studying His Word, we find out that He does talk to us in a small, quiet voice. It's up to us to take the time to listen.

In order to love God, we need to know God. In order to know God, we need to read His Word. It's that simple. There is no shortcut.

USE YOUR TONGUE WISELY

With the tongue we praise our Lord and Father, and with it we curse men who have been made in God's likeness (James 3:9).

Okay, here is some hardcore honesty. Before I had a relationship with God, I didn't give a second thought to talking badly about a family member, co-worker, or total stranger. If they did something stupid (in my opinion) or something that made me mad, I felt obligated to talk about them behind their backs to anyone who would listen. I wasn't doing anything wrong; they were the ones who did something they shouldn't have.

Knowing God on a personal level allows us to know what He expects of us—and He certainly does not want us cursing His children whom He made in His image. We know what happens when we talk negatively about someone over and over again—the offense gets bigger and bigger in our minds. We dwell on it. We keep it fresh in our minds so we never get over it. And Satan loves that!

Let's use the fruit of the spirit called self-control to not curse others but instead use our tongues to glorify and edify the Father and His Kingdom.

FORGIVE

Bear with each other and forgive whatever grievances you may have against one another. Forgive as the Lord forgave you (Colossians 3:13).

In conversations with Christians, I have heard that the most difficult thing for some of them to do is forgive another person who has hurt them. And it appears that the closer they are to the person who violated them, the more difficult it is to forgive. When someone told John Wesley, the founder of Methodism, "I just can't forgive that person. They hurt me too badly," Wesley replied, "Then I hope you never sin."

My friend and I had a long discussion about this the other night, and we decided that almost always—with very few exceptions—it is more stressful for the person who does not forgive than for the person who needs the forgiveness. Not forgiving gives the person power over our emotions. It also lets God know that we don't truly believe He is capable of healing our wound.

Forgiveness does not mean the offense was okay. Forgiving others means we appreciate God's forgiveness. It means we love Jesus Christ and what He did for our salvation—that we are going to rely on His Word and on Him to free us from the hurt.

PAY ATTENTION

We must pay more careful attention, therefore, to what we have heard, so that we do not drift away (Hebrews 2:1).

When I was young, a popular saying was, "Put your thinking caps on." Teachers used this saying often when students were having trouble concentrating (perhaps right after recess), when they were asked to review past lessons, and especially when they were about to take a test. The teacher wanted the students to be at the top of their game so they could recall the knowledge necessary to tackle what was coming their way.

I was a student the first day I walked into class. I was a student before I read any of the textbooks. However, I found it much easier to pass the tests once I read and studied the material. In the same way, we can be Christians before we read the Bible. But it's a lot simpler to pass the tests once we read the book.

In order to overcome whatever life throws our way, we need to put on our Christian thinking caps. We need to recall all that we have learned from Biblical teachings and our own reading and study of the Bible. We need to use the knowledge we've gained so that we do not drift away from God. It is only by recalling what we've learned and know about God and His Son, our Savior, that we are able to stand the tests of each day.

RESIST YOUR PAST SINS

Submit yourselves, then, to God. Resist the devil and he will flee from you (James 4:7).

When I first started speaking publicly about God and the wonderful things He has done in my life, Satan was all over me. He attacked with a vengeance. He put in my mind that I wasn't a good enough person to speak about God. Satan loved to place my sins of the past and present in my mind. He often reminded me how weak I am and how easily I could be persuaded to do what was wrong.

He would tell me my talk was irrelevant and my delivery was bad. I believed this evil one. I started adding to the negative talk—*You can't do this, Bev; who do you think you are?* Satan was celebrating when that happened. "Woohoo! She is bringing herself down. I don't have to spend any more energy to do it. She's doing it all by herself! She'll be done with this foolish witnessing in no time."

What Satan wasn't counting on was that I was reading the Bible every single day. I was arming myself with God's love, grace, and mercy. I was learning more and more about the sacrifice Jesus made for me! And God was putting loving Christian people in my life, and instead of doubting myself, I was becoming more confident in the Lord. I found that each time I resisted the devil, I got a little stronger. Each time I said, "No, Satan, you are not getting to me. I have on the armor of Christ," it became easier to do the right thing.

It is difficult to resist the devil because he knows so much about us and the temptations that can make us stumble. Know that each time you submit yourself to God and resist Satan, you too will become stronger and more confident.

GOD IS HERE

Be still and know that I am God (Psalm 46:10).

Shhhhhhhh ... be still. God's here. Isn't it wonderful to know God is always here?

My dad recently passed away after a very short battle with cancer. It seemed that once he was diagnosed, he became weaker and weaker by the minute. Within days, he was unable to walk on his own and needed help getting in and out of bed.

One afternoon, my brother, Wayne, had just put him in bed, and Dad said something to him that he couldn't hear. Wayne bent down over him and asked Dad to repeat it. At the same time, Wayne felt a very comforting pat on the back. He assumed it was his friend who had said he was coming to visit. It was about the time he was scheduled to arrive, and it was a familiar pat on the back—like the pat came from someone who knew him and wanted to reassure him that everything would be okay.

After Wayne responded to Dad, he stood up and looked behind him. No one was there. His friend had not yet arrived. Wayne told me it was then that he realized it had been God. It was God who gave him that familiar pat on the back to assure him He was there and that it would be okay.

There was an amazing peace that came from knowing that even in Dad's sickness that would end his life, God was there. And how loving of God to remind us.

DISTRIBUTE GOODNESS

Do not be overcome by evil, but overcome evil with good (Romans 12:21).

I remember being a young, stressed-out, working wife and mother not that many years ago. When I could fit in a lunch or dinner with my best friend, Chris, I gladly took advantage of that time with her. She always seemed more together and wiser than I was. We loved talking and listening to each other. There are many reasons why we have remained best friends for over thirty years now.

It seemed that I was always frustrated with people around me—my co-workers, clients, and family members. I would go on and on about the mistreatment and rudeness I endured at the hands of these people (a one-sided story to be certain), and at the end, Chris would calmly say, "Kill them with kindness."

I would try to explain, "But these people have been mean to me!" Chris would repeat, "Kill them with kindness."

Just this morning, twenty-five years later, with a much stronger faith and a greater understanding of God's word, I realized that Romans 12:21 says the same thing. When someone is rude and inconsiderate to us, we are not to be rude and inconsiderate in return, thereby adding to the evil. We are called by God to offer kindness, which will diffuse the evil and stop it from spreading. Evil will be replaced with goodness and God's love.

Whether you remember this idea as "kill them with kindness" or "overcome evil with good," try it. You'll be surprised at how wise God is (and how wise my friend Chris is, too).

ALWAYS SERVE THE LORD

Whatever you do, work at it with all your heart, as working for the Lord, not for men (Colossians 3:23).

One morning, I went in to work and found myself totally bored with the work around me. We had had a powerful Mission Team meeting at church the night before, and my heart and mind were with mission work. I checked my e-mail, and I had received a note from a friend on the Mission Team. I responded to her question, and I threw in, "I am bored with what I have to do today. I would rather be doing mission work." We discussed how our jobs seemed trivial and mundane—surely God wanted us to quit our jobs and spend every moment working for Him. Although neither of us could remember the Scripture at the time, we both knew there was Scripture reminding us that whatever we are doing, we should do it to the best of our ability in honor of God—even our jobs that seemed unimportant at the moment.

That afternoon, I received an e-mail, and this e-mail described how each person has a birthday Scripture and explained how it worked. I don't remember all the details, but I do remember that since my birthday is March 23, my birthday Scripture is Colossians 3:23—the *exact* Scripture my friend and I were talking about that morning.

Every job, every conversation, and every activity can glorify God if we do it to the best of our ability, with a good attitude, and with a serving heart.

A LIVING BIBLE

Do not merely listen to the word and so deceive yourselves. Do what it says (James 1:22).

Reading the Bible is a great start to living a Christian life. We certainly need to know what God's Word is in order to follow God's Word. Reading the Bible means nothing, however, if we don't put it into practice. We can't just read about love; we have to practice love. We can't just hear about forgiveness; we must forgive. We can't just read about the goodness of Jesus without sharing that goodness with others. We must act out the Bible—live the way it tells us to live. Reading a cookbook does no good unless we are willing to get out the mixing bowls and make something good to eat. Reading the Bible means nothing unless we are willing to put aside our own agenda and live like Jesus lived.

This would be easy if everyone around us lived according to God's Word. If everyone else was nice and kind, we could be nice and kind, too. If people offered us love and help when we needed it, then we could easily offer love and help in return. We all know that's not the way life in this world is. What we need to realize is that there are people out there who have never known love. There are people who have grown up with hatred and anger in their homes. There are so many reasons why people are unhappy, and we have no way of knowing what they have been through or what they have had to endure. It's up to us as Christians to do what the Bible says. It's up to us to start the trend. It's up to us to show Jesus' love in *all* situations. Love, kindness, forgiveness, and mercy must begin with us.

GOD'S PERFECT TIMING

The things I plan won't happen right away. Slowly, steadily, surely, the time approaches when the vision will be fulfilled. If it seems slow, do not despair for things will surely come to pass. Just be patient. They will not be overdue a single day (Habakkuk 2:3 NLT).

That Scripture sounds so beautiful when I read it. God has it all under control. His timing is perfect. Be patient. Why are these instructions so difficult to follow?

Should we be doing something while we are waiting and being patient? For instance, if we're looking for a job, do we hope God finds us one as we sit on the sofa and be patient? Do we trust He will make the phone ring, and the perfect offer will be on the other line? Do we send out dozens of resumes and pray that the job God wants us to have will be the only response we will get? If we don't hear from a particular company, do we assume that's not the job He wants us to have, or do we call every day because

God wants us to be enthusiastic and willing to work for what we want?

God wants us to put every effort into obtaining our goals. We are not to expect a job offer if we haven't applied for a job. We are to work for our dreams and passions, putting our best effort into all that we do. We are to never give up. We are to wait patiently for the results of our hard work, knowing that God's timing will be perfect.

PEACE AMIDST TROUBLE

I have told you these things, so that in me you may have peace. In this world you will have trouble. But take heart! I have overcome the world (John 16:33).

In the few mission trips I've been on, I have gotten a clear picture that God provides peace among trouble. Hurricane Katrina left total devastation in a huge area of the southern United States. Yet people whom I met in Mississippi and Louisiana were thankful and grateful for the help they received from people they didn't even know. In spite of the damage that was done, they felt blessed because of the love and support of so many who reached out to them. In Guatemala, I witnessed some of the most passionate worship I have ever seen. The village we stayed in doesn't have the water they need to keep them healthy. But they love Jesus Christ and the salvation He offers.

Look at what happened after the September 11, 2001 terrorist attacks in New York City. The people of the

United States pulled together in extreme ways. Money was donated, help was given, and love was displayed.

Each time something horrific happens, God counteracts it through His Son—His Son, who came to save the world. If you ever find yourself wondering, "Where was God when this happened?" look for love, and that's where you will find God.

PREPARE TO WITNESS

But in your hearts set apart Christ as Lord. Always be prepared to give an answer to everyone who asks you to give the reason for the hope that you have. But do this with gentleness and respect (1 Peter 3:15).

I can't count the number of times I have missed a wonderful opportunity to witness for the Lord simply because I didn't have the words to speak. My first husband died in 1999 of a massive heart attack. I was a thirty-nine-year-old widow with two young daughters. People ask me all the time how I got through that. For years, I missed the chance to say, "Only through the mercy and love of the Lord." As simple as those words are, I just didn't know how to speak them. I said things like, "Oh, you just do" or "I didn't have much choice." But the truth is, we don't just get through rough times, and we do have a choice. I could have very easily chosen to be angry and bitter after my husband passed away. However, with God surrounding me with His love and with His loving people, the choice to move on in His hope was the easiest choice. What a tragedy that people have missed that message because I was not prepared with the right words.

I encourage you to write a sentence or a paragraph about why your hope is in the Lord. Write down events in your life that were affected by the love and grace of our Savior, Jesus Christ. Write down what it means to you to have given your life to Jesus. On a regular basis, look at what you wrote down so that you will be ready to share the good news of Jesus Christ with gentleness and respect.

GOD SAID SO

Do not seek revenge or bear a grudge against one of your people, but love your neighbor as yourself. I am the Lord (Leviticus 19:18).

Oh, the energy we waste trying to get even—the effort we throw away by holding a grudge. The funny thing is, most of the time, the other person doesn't even know anything is going on. We are fretting over what they did to us and how we can get even, and they are living their lives like nothing is going on. We are plotting and planning for our big revenge, and they are living a fun, stress-free life.

Do you remember the first time you said something and as soon as the words came out of your mouth, you thought, "Oh no, I've become my mother (or father)?" For me, it was a time when I gave my daughter instructions, and she asked, "Why?" Not being able to come up with a great reason right away, I used the old, familiar phrase, "Because I said so, that's why."

The Bible is filled with Scripture addressing forgiveness and having loving hearts. Leviticus 19:18 is my favorite, because at the end it says, "I am the Lord." To me, that's the same as God saying, "Because I said so." I can't think of a better reason to forgive than because our Heavenly Father says so.

CONTINUE DOING GOOD

So don't get tired of doing what is good. Don't get discouraged and give up, for we will reap a harvest of blessing at the appropriate time (Galatians 6:9 NLT).

Do you ever feel like you are the only one following the rules? Do you feel like you're the only one who is nice to others or the only one doing more than your share of work? Sometimes it seems to be a burden to do what's right in a world where people tend to be inconsiderate of others—a world where it truly appears that nice guys finish last.

I work with the public, and I am nice to people. It's in my job description. When I go shopping or make an inquiry on the phone, as a customer, I expect the same treatment in return. That doesn't always happen. When I'm the customer service representative, I have to be nice to customers, even when they are grumpy. When I'm the customer, I have to be nice, even when the clerk is grumpy. I've asked myself more than once, "When do I get to be the grumpy one?" The answer to that is never, because I may be the only glimpse of Jesus the person I'm speaking to will get that day.

Whenever we begin to feel discouraged or feel like giving up, remember that God sees what we are doing, and He promises us a harvest of His blessings.

GOD OF HOPE

May the God of hope fill you with all joy and peace as you trust in Him, so that you may overflow with hope by the power of the Holy Spirit (Romans 15:13).

Life is worth living when we have hope in the Lord. There is so much anger, hatred, and chaos in the world; without hope, it would be difficult to have joy. There is so much tragedy all around us that without hope in God, it would be impossible to know peace.

When I first began establishing a relationship with God, I had no idea what He had to offer. I believed in Him and felt the desire to serve Him by serving His children. I had no idea what I would receive in return. In the beginning, I didn't know what inner joy and peace were—and perhaps neither do you. The best way I can describe it is this: have you ever had a perfect day where everything seemed to go just right? Maybe you can recall when everything felt good. I have heard these times described as "fleeting moments of euphoria." That's how I feel every day now that I know and trust God. When I first started feeling this way, I wondered when it would end. But with the God of hope in my heart, the moments aren't fleeting anymore. There is constant peace and joy.

This Scripture is packed full of wisdom. God offers hope to each one of us through the power of the Holy Spirit. If we want to have peace and joy, we must trust that God will be there for us in every situation. Hope, joy, peace, trust—He offers all of this to us simply because He loves us. His Son made the sacrifice, and we get to enjoy the benefits.

Thank You, Father, Son, and Holy Spirit for the hope you freely offer to each one of us. Amen.

NOW IS RIGHT

*Whoever watches the wind will not plant; whoever
looks at the clouds will not reap* (Ecclesiastes 11:4).

Do any of these statements sound familiar to you? "We'll
get married when we have more money." "We'll have
babies when my career is established and I feel more
settled." "We'll go on that mission trip when our children
are older." "We'll be on a committee at church when our
children are not involved in so many things." "We'll be
more open to God's call when we retire." "We wish we had
done more when we were younger and could get around
better."

If we wait for our lives to be just right, we will never be the
servants God wants us to be. He's calling you now to plant
and to reap. When is "the perfect time?" When God calls
you. *Shhhhh*—listen. He's calling you now.

DENY EVIL DESIRES

As obedient children, do not conform to the evil desires you had when you lived in ignorance (1 Peter 1:14).

Breaking old habits can be the very thing that keeps us from living the abundant life God wants us to live. Reverting to old ways of living may be what denies us a true relationship with God. Some of the things I did before I had a relationship with the Lord are things that I am not proud of at all. I was known to not forgive, spread rumors, seek revenge, lie, use the Lord's name in vain, drink way too much, and more.

Knowing God and knowing that Jesus was sacrificed for my sins makes me want to live in obedience. Because God loves me and knows what's best for me, I want to follow His will for me. Sometimes when my defenses get weak, I'm tired, I'm facing difficult situations, or I'm not studying the Bible like I should, the old habits slowly creep into my mind. I find myself tempted to revert back to the old ways.

It's important that we recognize when this happens so we can ask Jesus to forgive us for our thoughts and ask Him to lead us from the temptation. It's perfectly fine to admit to God that we are weak. He already knows it anyway. He wants to hear it from us, because then He knows we are aware of it and we want to break the cycle of our old ways. Ask God to help you be obedient.

RENEWED THROUGH CHRIST

But those who hope in the Lord will renew their strength. They will soar on wings like eagles; they will run and not grow weary, they will walk and not grow faint (Isaiah 40:31).

In June of 2006, I led a mission trip to New Orleans to help with Hurricane Katrina relief efforts. We were responsible for going into homes that had not yet been touched since the hurricane in August of 2005. We took everything out of the homes, placed it alongside the street for pickup, tore the drywall off of the walls and ceiling, and took up the flooring. We were to take every room down to the studs. (You can see pictures of this on my website at www.WeSpeakCommunications.com.) The majority of us were not physical laborers or young people. Among us were teachers, secretaries, a college dean, retirees, and other sedentary individuals.

The first day we worked, the temperature reached 100 degrees. We were from Ohio, and in this first week of June, we had barely hit eighty degrees. We were not used to that kind of heat. Yet we worked for eight hours that day. The next day, we got up and did it again. We did this for five days. At the end of each day, we would look at each other in amazement as we realized what we had accomplished. We told each other over and over again that it was through the strength of God that we could do what we did. When we grew tired and weary, the Lord renewed our strength.

OBEDIENCE

When he had finished speaking, he said to Simon, "Put out into deep water, and let down the nets for a catch." Simon answered, "Master, we've worked hard all night and haven't caught anything. But because you say so, I will let down the nets" (Luke 5:4–5).

I will do it because you say so. I'm sure my parents would have like to have heard that a few times when I was growing up. It signifies such obedience and respect.

How many times have we gotten a word or a prodding thought from God and questioned what the outcome would be? We want to know what our reward will be or what the end result will be. I can't help but believe that each one of us has asked the question, "But why?" I will admit that I have.

"Okay, God, I hear you asking me to help the people in Haiti. But why? I don't have very much—what difference could I make?"

"You want me to visit a shut-in? But why? I barely know her."

"I should call my neighbor who lives alone? But why? Does he need something?"

"You want me to offer to babysit for children of a single mom? But why? She has family in town."

That question "but why?" was a question I asked over and over again when I was debating whether or not to go to Guatemala a few years ago. I wanted God to give me a clear picture as to how I would be able to help. I wanted to know what my part in the mission would be and how I could possibly make a difference. I wanted to know the ending before I committed to the beginning. I should have been saying, "Because You say so—that's why I'm going." I went to Guatemala, and I still to this day don't know why. Here's a news flash—sometimes when we answer God's call, it has nothing to do with us. It may be years before the effects of our obeying God come to fruition. Or it may impact someone's life in a way that doesn't affect us, and we may never know it. It's not about you or me. It is about obeying God.

SHARE THE GOOD NEWS

The most important thing is that I complete my mission, the work that the Lord Jesus gave to me—to tell people the Good News about God's Grace (Acts 20:24 NCV).

Witnessing—now there's something that's uncomfortable. For some reason, it seems that our nature is to keep Jesus to ourselves. That's pretty selfish of us, though. That's keeping a good thing a secret. If we found a great place to eat where the food was excellent, large portions were served, and the prices were low, we would share that information for sure! Why is it so uncomfortable for us to share our faith with the same people with whom we share the exciting news of a good restaurant?

Part of growing and maturing in Christianity is showing love. The way we show love is to invite others into the family of Christ. What better gift can we give to our neighbor than an invitation to join us on Sunday morning in the fellowship and feeling of belonging that we enjoy so much?

Sharing the good news of Jesus Christ is what God has called us to do, and whenever we are obedient, God rewards us richly. As a matter of fact, in 2 Peter 1:11, we will hear God's promise: "For if you do these things you will never fall and you will receive a rich welcome into the eternal kingdom of our Lord and Savior Jesus Christ." That sounds like a fabulous way to enter the kingdom—with a rich welcome. Not with "Hi, how ya doin'?" but with *"Welcome!* Come on in! We've been waiting for you! Hey Jesus—look who's here!" And by the way, this is exactly how we should be welcoming people into our church.

GOD IS GOOD

Taste and see that the Lord is good, blessed is the man who takes refuge in him (Psalm 34:8).

When my daughter was young, she was afraid to try new things—and that included trying new things to eat. I would take a bite of something—say, strawberry cheesecake—and say, "Yum. This is so good!"

She would inevitably ask, "What does it taste like?"

I would say, "It tastes like strawberry cheesecake, and it is good."

That answer never quite satisfied her. She would continue her skepticism by asking, "But what does strawberry cheesecake taste like?" She was trying to get a guarantee that it was something she would like before she tried it. Eventually, I would convince her to take a small bite. I knew the only way to find out if something tastes good is to try it for yourself.

That's the only way we will know that the Lord is good—to try Him for ourselves. We can read what He did for Abraham, Moses, Mary, Peter, John, Paul, the blind, the sick, and all the others in the Bible. But the only way to truly know that the Lord is good is by inviting Him into our lives, trusting Him for all our needs, and accepting His love for us.

Taste and you will see that the Lord is good!

PROCLAIM THE LORD

Immediately the rooster crowed the second time. Then Peter remembered the word Jesus had spoken to him. "Before the rooster crows twice you will disown me three times." And he broke down and wept (Mark 14:72).

I stand in utter amazement every time I read that Peter denied knowing Jesus. Peter saw Jesus walk on water. Peter was an eyewitness to Jesus healing the sick, and Peter watched as Jesus calmed the storm. How could it have been so easy for Peter to deny knowing the Son of God? Perhaps he was afraid—would the soldiers kill him, too?

In the United States, there is little fear of persecution by announcing Jesus as our Savior. Yet many of us, by saying nothing at all, deny Jesus' existence. What are we afraid of—offending someone? Are we afraid someone will question us and we won't have all the answers? Do we think we aren't worthy to speak of the Lord? Our fears may be different than Peter's, but I believe our denial still comes from being afraid.

Peter wept when he realized what he had done. I challenge you to take every opportunity available to publicly proclaim Jesus as your Savior. We have nothing to fear. Jesus is on our side!

SEND ME

Then I heard the voice of the Lord saying, "Whom shall I send? And who will go for us?" And I said, "Here I am. Send me" (Isaiah 6:8).

This is the attitude every Christian should have. Every person who loves the Lord should want to serve Him by serving His people.

For me my first response, the response that comes most naturally is, "Yes, send me." I never thought it was a bad thing. I've had some amazing experiences by saying yes. When I was raising my daughters and working full-time, however, I remember reading a magazine article that addressed the situation differently. This article gave this advice: place a big piece of paper with the word no on it right next to your telephone. The idea was that when someone called you on the phone to ask you to bake cookies, to work at the concession stand at the football game, to cook for a funeral dinner, to watch the children in the nursery, etc., you would stare at the paper while the other person was talking, and it would give you the courage to say, "No!" Don't get me wrong—"just say no" has a place in our society, but I don't think it should be our own personal mission statement. I say you should put a large piece of paper by your phone and write the word *yes* on it. We all know the most dreaded place to be during the game is on the bench—it just wrinkles your skirt. At the end of the day, if my skirt is wrinkled and my behind is sore, I want it to be because I played the game, not because I sat on the bench along the sidelines and watched.

If you're not sure you are up to the task, I say you should err on the side of saying yes. You will either find something new you can do for the Lord, or you'll find something you can check off of your list and leave for someone else next time. Practice saying it a few time so you'll be ready: "Here I am, send me. *Here I am, Lord—send me!*"

Okay, you're ready! Go out and serve!